THE DISTRIBUTION OF FARM SUBSIDIES

CHARLES L. SCHULTZE

THE DISTRIBUTION OF FARM SUBSIDIES:
WHO GETS THE BENEFITS?

A Staff Paper

THE BROOKINGS INSTITUTION
Washington, D.C.

THE BROOKINGS INSTITUTION is an independent organization devoted to nonpartisan research, education, and publication in economics, government, foreign policy, and the social sciences generally. Its principal purposes are to aid in the development of sound public policies and to promote public understanding of issues of national importance.

The Institution was founded on December 8, 1927, to merge the activities of the Institute for Government Research, founded in 1916, the Institute of Economics, founded in 1922, and the Robert Brookings Graduate School of Economics and Government, founded in 1924.

The general administration of the Institution is the responsibility of a Board of Trustees charged with maintaining the independence of the staff and fostering the most favorable conditions for creative research and education. The immediate direction of the policies, program, and staff of the Institution is vested in the President, assisted by an advisory committee of the officers and staff.

In publishing a study, the Institution presents it as a competent treatment of a subject worthy of public consideration. The interpretations and conclusions in such publications are those of the author or authors and do not necessarily reflect the views of the other staff members, officers, or trustees of the Brookings Institution.

FOREWORD

Our massive and complex system of agricultural subsidies clearly ranks among the more important programs of the federal government. Its total cost in 1969, measured as the sum of direct outlays of federal funds and the amount represented by higher prices paid by consumers of agricultural products, roughly equaled the cost in the same year of all federal, state, and local welfare programs, including Medicaid.

Who are the beneficiaries of the subsidy program? Are subsidies effective in protecting the living standards of small, low-income farmers? Of each subsidy dollar, how much do efficient, fairly well-to-do large-scale farmers receive? After describing the origins and present structure of the various federal farm programs, Charles L. Schultze in this staff paper analyzes the distribution of benefits by size of farm and income group, and investigates the influence of subsidies on the net returns and value of farmland. He concludes that, regardless of their original purposes, federal subsidies are a poor device for helping large numbers of low-income farmers.

Mr. Schultze, now a Brookings Senior Fellow and Professor of Economics at the University of Maryland, was Director of the Bureau of the Budget from 1965 to 1968. He is indebted to Nancy C. Wilson, who carried out the complex calculations the analysis required, and to the many agricultural economists, both in government and private life, whose comments improved the manuscript. Among them he is particularly grateful to James Bonnen, John Schnittker, M. L. Upchurch, and Bruce Johnson, whose advice was invaluable.

He also acknowledges with gratitude the assistance of Evelyn P. Fisher, who ensured that the analysis remained faithful to the source data, and to Alice M. Carroll, who edited the manuscript.

The project was carried out as part of the Brookings program of research on public expenditures and budgeting, which is supported by a grant from the Carnegie Corporation of New York.

The views expressed here are those of the author. They should not be attributed to the persons consulted during the analysis or the preparation of the manuscript, to the Carnegie Corporation, or to the trustees, officers, or staff members of the Brookings Institution.

KERMIT GORDON
President

February 1971
Washington, D.C.

CONTENTS

Tables

Figures

CHAPTER ONE

INTRODUCTION

Between 1956 and 1970, federal budget outlays for farm price support programs and related direct payments to farmers averaged $3.1 billion per year. In the last three years of this period, 1968 through 1970, annual budget outlays averaged $5 billion. These costs of supporting farm prices and incomes were paid by the taxpayer. But consumers also pay, through higher prices, part of the costs of farm price support programs. Federal farm programs are designed—recently through output restrictions, in earlier years through loans and purchases of farm products—to raise the price of farm products above what a free market would have yielded. While estimates vary, actual farm prices in recent years would have been perhaps 15 percent lower had federal price support programs not been in effect. At supported prices the value of farm marketings in 1969 amounted to over $47 billion. With prices 15 percent lower, the same volume of farm output could have been purchased for about $7 billion less. Some $1.5 billion of this reduction would represent lower prices paid by farmers themselves in buying feed, seed, and livestock. Lower prices for exports would represent another $1 billion. Nonfarm consumers, therefore, paid in recent years about $4.5 billion more for the farm products they purchased than they would have had there been no federal price support programs.[1]

Farm price support and related programs thus cost the taxpayer some $5 billion per year in budgetary outlays, and consumers of food and fiber some $4.5 billion in higher food prices—although the latter figure may overstate somewhat the long-term price-raising effects of farm support programs. The total transfer from consumers and taxpayers, in the range of $9 to $10 billion, compares with a total federal, state, and local cost of various public assistance

1. With output restrictions removed and prices lower, more food and fiber would be produced and consumed. As a consequence farmers' cash receipts from marketing would not fall by the same percentage as prices.

(welfare) programs, including Medicaid, of slightly over $10 billion in 1969. Procurement, operation, and maintenance of the nation's strategic nuclear forces cost about $9 billion in fiscal 1969.

In terms of their cost, farm subsidies clearly rank among the more important public programs. They have a noticeable effect on many vital factors in the national economy—the allocation of resources, the location of population and industry, the balance of payments, and so on. One of the major impacts of farm subsidies is upon income distribution, which raises the question "Who gets the subsidies?" Specifically, to what extent do farm programs represent a transfer of income from a relatively affluent urban population to a relatively depressed and low-income farm community? While such a transfer would not necessarily in itself justify the programs, it would at least indicate an effort to distribute income in a way that most people would consider equitable.

In 1969 the median family income of the nonfarm population was $9,600, that of farm families $6,400, or some 33 percent lower. The transfer of substantial sums from the nonfarm to the farm population would thus seem likely to distribute income more evenly. This is not the case, however. Farm subsidies are not distributed in accordance with income levels—poor families receiving the most assistance and rich families the least. Rather they tend, at least roughly, to be distributed in proportion to the volume of production on each farm. The more a farm produces, the greater the value of price supports. Moreover, most of the cash payments a farmer receives from the government depend on the size of his acreage allotment or his production, both of which vary directly with the size of his farm.

A relatively small number of large farmers produce the bulk of agricultural goods sold in the United States. Three-fourths of the sales of farm products are made from 568,000 farms with annual sales of $20,000 or more. Those farms comprise only 19 percent of all farms. The average income of their operators, from farm and nonfarm sources, was $19,900 in 1968 and $20,900 in 1969. Since farm subsidies accrue roughly in proportion to sales, it follows that the bulk of subsidies go to that fifth of farmers with the highest average income. At the other end of the scale are 1.5 million small farmers with annual sales of less than $5,000 and annual incomes, from farm and nonfarm sources, averaging about $7,900.[2] They account for only 5 percent of farm sales and a correspondingly small fraction of farm subsidy benefits.

Most farm subsidy programs are vested not in the farmer as an individual but in the land on his farm. The farmer's benefits are based on his acreage

2. A large number of part-time farmers are included in this total. The average net income of this group from farming is only $1,300.

allotment or acreage history. This determines how many acres he must refrain from planting, as a condition for participation in the program. Should the farmer leave the farm, he cannot directly take his subsidy with him. The subsidy privileges remain with the land. As a general rule, the land retains its acreage allotment and its acreage history, whoever owns it. Naturally, therefore, the value of the annual subsidy tends to get reflected, at least partially, in the price of the farmland.[3] In combination with a number of other factors, this capitalization process has tended to drive the price of farmland up. As a consequence, the chief benefits of farm subsidies have accrued to those who purchased land before subsidies became prevalent. Farmers buying land in later years, however—younger farmers and those expanding their acreage to take advantage of technological advances—have received less advantage from the farm programs. The benefits of higher prices and direct subsidies have at least partly been offset by the added costs incurred because of higher land prices. And farmers who have rented land have found many of the benefits disappearing in higher rental payments to landlords.

Indeed, at the limit, a subsidy attached to land eventually ends up granting no benefits to farmers. To the extent that the value of the subsidy is capitalized into land prices, the higher carrying costs soak up the annual subsidy, as land gradually changes hands over the years. But since subsidy values are frozen into the price of land, any attempt to reduce or remove them would leave recent purchasers of land with incomes below what they would have been before the subsidy program started and confront them with a capital loss. Paradoxically, therefore, after a number of years have passed, such programs end up transferring little net income to the second generation of recipients, but at the same time become so frozen into asset values that their removal would bring substantial hardship.

Whatever the advantages or disadvantages of the farm subsidy program, it is not a welfare program in the sense of transferring income to low-income farm families. The bulk of the subsidies accrue to that small group of farmers with net incomes averaging $20,000. And because the value of the subsidy tends to get reflected in farmland prices, the subsidies are gradually translated into capital gains for long-term holders of land, while recent purchasers and renters receive a much smaller benefit, losing at least part of the subsidy in higher carrying costs or rents.

---

3. Cotton and tobacco allotments may be sold. Thus the capitalized value of the subsidy program may be separated from the land, and the farmer can realize that value without selling the land itself.

CHAPTER TWO

WHENCE FARM PRICE SUPPORT PROGRAMS?

Throughout most of his history, first as hunter and then as farmer, man has struggled to wrest a greater supply of food from a grudging nature. Increased agricultural productivity meant at first a more nearly assured victory in the fight for survival, then a better and more varied diet. Later, as man became able to produce more than the needs of his immediate family, food surpluses made it possible to free increasing numbers of people to develop commerce, industry, and the arts.

In the developing countries, where two-thirds of the world's people live, securing cheap and abundant food supplies continues to be a major pre-occupation of governments and a prerequisite for economic advance. But in the United States since the 1920s and more recently in Western Europe, this state of affairs has been inverted. Excess agricultural production and rapidly rising farm productivity have become chronic problems for presidents and prime ministers, congresses and parliaments, farm organizations and inter-national conferences. National policies and international agreements have been adopted to restrict the production and raise the price of food and fiber. National budgets provide large subsidies for farmers as an inducement to reduce their output and as a means of raising farm prices and farm incomes above what the market would otherwise provide.

Four factors have combined in advanced industrial countries to change the age-old objective of increasing agricultural production to one of restricting production: a rapid rate of growth in agricultural productivity; a low price elasticity of demand for farm products; a decline in the income elasticity of demand for farm products, accompanying economic growth; and an apparent social and economic limit to the rate at which resources can be transferred to nonagricultural uses.

The rapid growth in agricultural productivity increases the supply of farm output that a given volume of resources can produce. A decline in the income elasticity of demand reduces the rate of growth in demand for that output and a low price elasticity accentuates the fall in farm income that a rapidly increasing supply occasions. The limited rate of egress from agriculture means that low incomes do not drive out excess resources from farming fast enough, so that low farm prices and incomes persist. In short, agricultural output increases faster than demand, but the surplus of resources stays in farm production rather than shifting to other industries. Unfortunately, the application of the wonders of modern technology on the farm produces not prosperity but poverty for a substantial number of the farm population.

Productivity

The application of modern technology and the substitution of machinery and fertilizer for land and labor have radically reduced the manpower requirements for agricultural production in the United States. Acreage yields have also risen rapidly. Moreover, as Table 1 illustrates, the rise in yield per acre and output per man-hour has sharply accelerated in recent years. Overall measures of farm productivity show the same pattern. Total input productivity—that is, farm output divided by a summary measure of all inputs, including land, labor, and capital—rose at an average annual rate of 0.5 percent per year from the period just before World War I to the period just prior to

Table 1. Labor Requirements and Yields of Selected Farm Products in the United States, Various Years

Product	Measure	1910-14	1935-39	1964-68[a]
Corn	Man-hours per 100 bushels	135.0	108.0	8.0
	Bushels per acre	26.0	26.0	73.0
Wheat	Man-hours per 100 bushels	106.0	67.0	11.0
	Bushels per acre	14.0	13.0	27.0
Potatoes	Man-hours per ton	25.0	20.0	4.0
	Hundredweight per acre	60.0	70.0	207.0
Cotton	Man-hours per bale	276.0	209.0	32.0
	Pounds per acre	201.0	226.0	506.0
Milk	Man-hours per hundredweight	3.8	3.4	1.0
	Hundredweight per cow	38.4	44.0	85.2
Cattle	Man-hours per hundredweight	4.6	4.2	2.2
Chickens	Man-hours per hundredweight	9.5	9.0	3.7
Turkeys	Man-hours per hundredweight	31.4	23.7	1.4

Source: U.S. Department of Agriculture (USDA), *Agricultural Statistics, 1969*, p. 458.
a. Preliminary figures.

World War II. In the thirty years since then, the average yearly growth rate has more than tripled, rising to 1.6 percent. As total input productivity rose, output per unit of labor rose even more rapidly, reflecting the substitution of capital for labor. For the United States farm economy as a whole, man-hour requirements per unit of output fell by 1.8 percent per year from 1910-14 to 1940-44. Since then the man-hour requirements per unit have declined at a 5.9 percent annual rate.

Demand for Farm Products

While the adoption of modern technology and rising productivity have sharply accelerated the supply of farm products that can be produced by a given volume of resources, the rate of growth in the demand for farm products has fallen. In poor countries, initial increases in living standards are still reflected substantially in better diets and greater food consumption. But as productivity and incomes rise, a smaller and smaller proportion of the income increase is used to buy food. In a country with living standards as high as the United States, only a very small part of further rises in income finds its way into an increased demand for food. Income elasticities of food demand in countries at different stages of economic development are evident in the following comparison:[1]

Richer nations	Elasticity	Poorer nations	Elasticity
United States	0.08	Italy	0.42
Canada	0.15	Ireland	0.23
Germany	0.25	Greece	0.49
France	0.25	Spain	0.56
Britain	0.24	Portugal	0.60

In several of the poorer countries of Europe, a 10 percent rise in income is accompanied by a 4 to 5 percent increase in food consumption, whereas in the United States such a rise increases food demand by less than 1 percent. Even with continued prosperity and steady growth in per capita income, the demand for food in the United States grows only slightly faster than population. The elasticity of demand in the industrial countries of Western Europe is slightly greater but still quite low.

1. Leo V. Mayer and others, *Farm Programs for the 1970's,* CAED Report 32 (Iowa State University, Center for Agricultural and Economic Development, 1968), p. 4, citing data from Organization for Economic Cooperation and Development, *Agriculture and Economic Growth, 1965.*

Given the low income elasticity of demand for food, sharp increases in farm productivity tend to increase the supply of farm products more rapidly than demand. The next factor in the problem then appears: a low price elasticity of demand. The excess supply of agricultural resources forces prices down. But the increase in food consumption in response to lower prices is also quite low. To clear the market of relatively modest increases in supply takes large decreases in farm prices. In a wealthy country, therefore, rapid rises in productivity must lead either to a rapid withdrawal of resources from farming or to depressed farm prices and incomes.

Withdrawing Resources from Farming

Despite the very rapid adoption of modern technology and the growth of large-scale farming, agriculture in the United States is still a family business, employing relatively few workers outside the family. Of the 4.7 million people employed on farms in 1968, only 1.2 million, or 25 percent, were hired workers; the rest were farm operators and family workers. Unlike an industrial concern, the typical farm enterprise facing a declining demand for its products cannot lay off 10 or 20 percent of its workers and adjust the work force to the market. The "labor force" of all except the very large farmer is in large part a fixed cost that represents the farmer's and his family's labor and that cannot be adjusted up or down. In the short run, output tends to be maintained regardless of market conditions. Withdrawing labor resources from farming is most often, in a free market, a matter of families leaving the farm. Necessarily this is a slow and painful process, both absolutely and in comparison to production adjustments in industrial enterprises. (In perhaps the majority of cases the land and capital stay in farming, as farms are consolidated into larger units.)

Moreover, a depressed market for agricultural products does not weaken the individual farmer's incentive to increase mechanization, to adopt modern technology, and to employ higher yielding seed. As far as he is concerned, techniques that lower costs and increase the output from a given acreage are not made less attractive by a weak market, over which he has no control. Indeed, the period of greatest farm modernization and mechanization has been precisely the period of excess supply, and that excess has been translated primarily into an excess in labor rather than a balance of all agricultural resources. This phenomenon is, of course, exacerbated by federal supply management programs and price support programs. Prices are guaranteed and output is restricted by the imposition of limits on the acreage a farmer may plant. He has an incentive to increase output by intensifying capital inputs on his limited acreage, and, in effect, a guaranteed minimum price for the resulting output increase.

The process of farm labor exodus has, all things considered, been quite dramatic in recent years. From the very earliest days of the nation up until the 1920s the number of farms increased steadily. By the mid-1920s, however, the expansion had come to an end, as the interaction of rising productivity and a low income elasticity of demand began to generate an excess supply of agricultural labor. The reduction in the number of farms was temporarily halted and reversed during the depression, as massive industrial unemployment forced people back to the farm. In the last thirty years the number of farms has been reduced by more than half, and the rate of decline has not slowed in recent years, as the following figures indicate:[2]

Year	Millions of farms	Year	Millions of farms
1850	1.4	1935	6.8
1870	2.7	1940	6.1
1900	5.7	1950	5.4
1920	6.5	1959	3.7
1930	6.3	1964	3.2

The decline in the number of farms and individual farmers, however, has not led to a significant fall in acreage. Much of the land given up by those leaving the farm has been purchased by those remaining.

Accelerating productivity growth, a low price and income elasticity of demand, and the difficulties of transferring the resulting oversupply of agricultural labor to other occupations have in the past forty years created the farm problem in the United States and other advanced industrial countries. Internal pressures have led, in most of those countries, to the adoption of policies designed to restrict farm output and raise farm prices and incomes above the levels yielded by a free market.

The Distribution of Farms by Size

Despite the fact that there are still more than 3 million farms in the United States, the bulk of farm production comes from a relatively small number of

2. U.S. Bureau of the Census, *Census of Agriculture, 1964, Statistics by Subjects,* Vol. 2, Chap. 1: *Farms and Land in Farms* (1967), Table 5, p. 15.

large-scale, efficient producers. The following percentages of total cash receipts received by farms in various brackets in 1939 and 1964 illustrate the point: [3]

	Size of farm (measured by volume of sales)							
Year	Smallest 10%	Smallest 20%	Smallest 33%	Smallest 50%	Largest 33%	Largest 20%	Largest 10%	Largest 1%
1939	2.5	4.7	7.8	11.9	75.0	62.3	45.2	18.0
1964	1.0	1.8	4.5	12.0	77.0	66.0	50.0	18.0

In both years about 65 percent of total farm receipts went to the 20 percent of farmers with the highest cash receipts. Only 12 percent of sales were made by farmers whose sales volume fell in the lower half of farm receipts.

While the relative distribution of receipts among large and small farmers has not changed sharply over the last twenty-five years—and probably not very much over an even longer period—the absolute size of farms has increased significantly since the 1920s. In the forty years between 1880 and 1920, the average size of the American farm increased by only 10 percent. In the next forty-four years, however, the average size rose by 138 percent. Those with 500 acres or more comprised 4 percent of the total in 1940 and 11 percent in 1964 (see Table 2).[4] Given the rapid increase in yields per acre during recent years, the volume of production on the average farm has expanded even more sharply than has the farm acreage. The absolute volume of production and sales on those large farms that account for the bulk of agricultural output has risen very steeply since the 1930s. The largest 20 percent of farms that accounted for roughly two-thirds of total farm sales in both 1939 and 1964 was, in terms of 1964 prices, composed of farms with sales of over $13,500 in 1939 and over $19,000 in 1964. In 1939 the average value of sales (adjusted to 1964 prices) from those farms was $27,100, and in 1964, $52,800, an increase of 95 percent in the real volume of marketings. The top 10 percent of farms in 1939 and 1964 accounted for about one-half of all farm sales; in 1939 their receipts (at 1964 price levels) averaged $37,200, and in 1964, $79,300.[5]

3. Lorenz curves derived from data in *Census of Agriculture, 1964,* Vol. 2, Chap. 6; *Value of Farm Products Sold and Economic Class of Farm* (1966), Tables 15 and 16; and U.S. Department of Agriculture (USDA), Economic Research Service (ERS), *Our 100,000 Biggest Farms: Their Relative Position in American Agriculture* (1964), Table 1, p. 2.

4. An important part of the increase in average farm size reflects a reduction in the number of small farms.

5. Derived from data in *Value of Farm Products Sold and Economic Class of Farm,* Tables 15 and 16; and *Our 100,000 Biggest Farms,* Table 1, p. 2. Receipts in 1939 at 1964 price levels" are based on the Department of Agriculture's index of "Prices Received by Farmers," *Agricultural Statistics, 1947,* p. 525, and *Agricultural Statistics, 1969,* p. 467.

Table 2. Distribution of Farms by Size of Acreage, Various Years

Year	Percentage of farms with			Average farm size (in acres)
	Less than 100 acres	Over 500 acres	Over 1,000 acres	
1880	55.1	2.6	0.7	134
1900	57.5	2.6	0.8	147
1920	58.6	3.4	1.0	149
1940	58.7	4.3	1.6	175
1950	56.0	5.6	2.3	216
1959	46.2	9.1	3.7	303
1964	43.1	11.3	4.6	352

Source: U.S. Bureau of the Census, *Census of Agriculture, 1964, Statistics by Subjects,* Vol. 2, Chap. 3: *Size of Farm* (1967), Tables 2 and 3, p. 241.

The absolute size of larger farms has expanded rapidly. Although they constitute only one-fifth to one-sixth of the total number of farms, in size and productivity they account for the bulk of agricultural output and marketings. And the net income of those farmers, after expenses, is also quite sizable, averaging close to $20,000 from farm and nonfarm sources (including non-money income from farm food and housing). Conversely, of course, small farmers, while they constitute the great majority in terms of numbers, produce only a small fraction of total farm output and receive only a modest fraction of total cash receipts. Necessarily, therefore, governmental programs that seek to alleviate the downward pressures on farm incomes by raising the value of farm cash receipts benefit primarily the large farmers who receive the bulk of those receipts. Moreover, the absolute size of the farms and the income level of those who receive the bulk of farm price support benefits has risen quite sharply over the life of the programs. Whatever their original objectives, the farm programs cannot be considered primarily a means of protecting the living standards of large numbers of low-income farmers.

Federal Farm Programs

From hindsight it seems clear that long-term problems of excess agricultural capacity began for the United States in the 1920s. These problems were recognized in the McNary-Haugen bills of 1927 and 1928 (vetoed twice by President Coolidge) and in the creation of the Federal Farm Board in 1929 with a $500 million revolving fund to engage in price stabilization operations. The depression of the 1930s saw the introduction of price support loan techniques and various supply management programs. But the special character of the farm problem was obscured by the pervasiveness of the depression. The subsequent sharp increase in demands on U.S. farms during World War II and the immediate postwar reconstruction period postponed the problem for almost a decade. Supplies were not excessive; farm incomes were rising. During this period, however, the concept of mandatory price supports was accepted with the enactment of programs for a number of major commodities.

The outbreak of the Korean War, with its inflationary consequences and worldwide anticipatory buying of commodities, further postponed the long-term consequences of rapidly rising farm productivity and low elasticities of demand. The buildup in Commodity Credit Corporation (CCC) stocks, which had begun in 1948 and 1949 as postwar inflationary demands tapered off, was reversed. Farm income rose sharply. It was not until the end of the Korean War that the problem of excess capacity began to make itself felt in a serious way.

The price support and supply management programs now in effect emerged from a long period of controversy and experimentation that began in the mid-1950s. As agricultural supplies rapidly outpaced demand, the maintenance of price supports at high levels forced the Commodity Credit Corporation to acquire a mounting inventory of agricultural products. Despite some reduction in price support levels after a politically charged congressional debate in 1954, CCC inventories and loan portfolios continued to rise sharply. The CCC investment in commodity inventories and price support loans, which had totaled $1.3 billion in June 1952, had by June 1955 reached $6.7 billion, and by June 1959, $7.7 billion. Although legislation had been enacted to create the soil bank, through which the government paid farmers to retire land from production, the volume of acreage retired was not sufficient to prevent a continuing production excess at supported prices and a consequent buildup in CCC stocks.

The incoming Kennedy administration, as one of several major steps in implementing its farm policy, raised support levels sharply on most basic crops. Farm income was increased, from an average of $2,832 per farm in 1956-60 to $3,749 in 1961-65. It also placed substantially greater emphasis on supply management programs, in order to raise farm income through output restrictions rather than continuing CCC acquisition of commodities. After experimenting with mandatory controls on output, the administration gradually came to rely on direct federal payments as a means of buying output restrictions from farmers. Direct payments currently provide a technique for keeping support levels high while reducing market prices to world levels—the payments make up the difference. Payments are also made on feed grains and wheat to purchase acreage restrictions, without which market prices would fall even lower. As a result of the acreage restrictions, farm output has been reduced sufficiently below sales that the Commodity Credit Corporation has been able to sell off a large part of the excessive inventories it had acquired under the high price supports of earlier years.

The farm programs that had gradually taken shape by 1965 were extended in that year's legislation for a five-year period. In November 1970 President Nixon signed a new three-year farm bill that continued, with certain changes, these basic farm price support programs. The new legislation places a limit of $55,000 per year on the amount an individual farm may receive on its wheat, feed grain, or cotton crop. This limitation, which will fall primarily on very large cotton farmers, will reduce direct government subsidies by an estimated $58 million per year. Other changes in the legislation provide somewhat more flexibility for farmers in deciding how they would use their land under voluntary acreage control programs. While it has been impossible to carry out a detailed analysis of the new law, there is little reason to believe its provisions would substantially affect the conclusions of this study. Because of the payment limitation, some 1,100 of the nation's 3 million farms will experience reductions in direct federal subsidies. But the distribution of subsidies by broad economic classes will probably not be sharply different from the estimates presented here.

Wheat, Feed Grains, and Cotton

For the three major crops—wheat, feed grains, and cotton—domestic market prices are now supported at or near world levels, rather than at the much higher prices initially set by the Kennedy administration. Producers who agree to restrict their acreage within, or in some cases below, their acreage allotments receive cash payments from the government, related directly or indirectly to their volume of production (payments may not exceed $55,000 on any one crop under the 1970 legislation). The cash the farmer receives for his crop is therefore a blend of market prices and government payments. Part of the direct payments for wheat are financed by processors, who must purchase marketing certificates proportional to the amount of wheat they process, at a 1969 price for certificates of 75 cents per bushel of wheat. Thus, some of the direct payments are borne by the consumer rather than the federal budget.

Direct payments for feed grains are the necessary price of getting producers to cooperate in reducing acreage by a sufficient amount to hold market prices at the support level. The same is true for wheat, but the level of payments is probably larger than needed simply to buy output restrictions. In other words, part of the wheat payments are pure income supplements, and part the price of purchasing supply controls. Direct payments are not needed to purchase output restrictions on cotton.[6] Traditionally, cotton producers have been willing to accept, by referendum vote, mandatory marketing quotas. Hence the current payments are primarily a means of maintaining cotton farmers' income while keeping prices near world levels.[7]

Tobacco, Rice, Peanuts, and Soybeans

Prices of tobacco, rice, peanuts, and soybeans are supported by CCC loans and purchases. Direct payments are not made. Acreage allotments and marketing quotas are used for the first three commodities to keep output at a level consistent with price support objectives, minimizing the need for direct CCC outlays. Acreage controls are not used in the soybean program.

Dairy Products

Dairy prices are supported by CCC purchases of manufactured milk products (butter, cheese, and dry milk) and through federal milk marketing orders that specify minimum prices of fluid milk in various dairy markets.

Sugar

Sugar prices are supported by the imposition of import quotas on foreign sugar and through acreage allotments to U.S. producers. As a consequence of this program, domestic raw sugar prices are maintained in the range of 6 to 8 cents per pound, while world sugar prices, in most years, range between 2 and 4 cents per pound.[8] In addition, sugar producers receive direct federal subsidies on their production, on the condition that they agree to maintain certain minimum wage levels for hired farm labor.

6. The 1966 and 1967 cotton programs did provide for substantial cuts in planted acreage, and special payments were made to secure this diversion. For these two years, crop production was held below consumption and exports in order to reduce the very substantial carryover that had been built up earlier. The reduction has now been accomplished.

7. Similar views on the relationship of direct payments to supply control objectives in the three major crop programs can be found in John A. Schnittker (former under secretary of agriculture), "The Distribution of Benefits from Existing and Prospective Farm Programs" (paper presented at the Symposium on Public Problems and Policies, Center for Agricultural and Economic Development, Iowa State University, May 27, 1969; processed).

8. This difference may overstate the subsidy, since the level of world market prices for sugar is artificially depressed by the fact that many major consuming nations have special arrangements with particular supplier nations.

Wool

Domestic wool producers receive a direct subsidy per pound of wool produced (27.2 cents per pound in 1969). No production controls are imposed.

Land Retirement

At the end of 1967, some 9 million acres were still retired from crop production under the old soil bank contracts. By January 1, 1970, almost all of these contracts had expired. Since 1967, about 4.5 million acres have been retired each year under the cropland adjustment and conversion programs. Such land retirement programs reduce potential farm output and help maintain prices above free market levels.

Agricultural Conservation Program (ACP)

The federal government makes direct payments under ACP to farmers for undertaking certain conservation practices—constructing water storage reservoirs, terracing, establishing vegetative cover, and the like. While the purpose of the program is the conservation of land, in practical terms it provides a subsidy to farmers, principally realized through an enhanced value and sales price of farmland.[9] This program's outlays are included among the direct farm subsidies examined in this study.

Program Costs

The transfer costs of the farm programs may be divided into two parts: a federal budgetary cost represented by the direct payments, and a cost to food and fiber consumers represented by the excess of supported farm prices over the level that would prevail in a free market.[10] During the past decade some of the costs shifted from the consumer to the budget as the direct payment programs for wheat, cotton, and feed grains were introduced—that is, market prices were reduced and the difference was made up through direct payments. But even in these three cases the resulting market prices are still above free market levels. Also during the past decade the total cost of the programs has increased, reflecting the higher support levels and income objectives adopted in the early 1960s.

9. For many years the administration in power has consistently attempted to reduce the size of this program. Among President Nixon's earliest budget recommendations was a proposal to abolish this program. But each year the Congress continues to appropriate some $200 million for ACP.

10. Farm subsidy programs involve economic costs as well as transfer costs. The economic, or welfare, costs represent the net loss of output to the economy as a whole that results from the reallocation of resources involved in the farm program. See Appendix A for a brief technical explanation of the two kinds of costs.

CHAPTER THREE

THE DISTRIBUTION OF BENEFITS
FROM FARM PROGRAMS

The benefits of farm price support programs are measured in this study principally in terms of the income farmers receive beyond what they would have received in the absence of the programs. This additional income is composed of both direct payments and price support benefits resulting from the support of farm market prices at levels above what a free market would yield.[1]

Distribution of Benefits by Size of Farm

There are several different ways of looking at the question "Who gets the benefits of farm programs?" James Bonnen has made extensive calculations of benefits under the major farm programs, ranking farms by the size of their acreage allotments and then indicating percentages of benefits going to farms in the various size classes. Bonnen uses Department of Agriculture data on acreage allotments distributed by size to compute the distribution of price support benefits; he assumes the benefits are proportional to acreage allotments, increasing as the allotments increase. The distribution of the direct payment benefits for wheat and feed grains he also calculates from Department of Agriculture data on payments to farmers in each allotment size class.

Bonnen's data, summarized in Table 3, show a significant concentration of benefits from price support programs among large farmers. With two exceptions—sugar beets and feed grain diversion payments—both price support and

1. The use of the term "price supports" can sometimes be confusing. In the case of corn, for example, farmers receive a market price for their crop, plus a direct government payment per bushel produced. These direct payments are called "price support payments," and the sum of the two (market price plus price support payments per bushel) is called "the support price." For purposes of clarity, price supports in this study refer to actions taken to hold actual market prices above free market levels. Payments received from the government (including the value of wheat certificates) are called "direct payments."

15

Table 3. Distribution of Farm Income and Commodity Program Benefits by Farm Size, Mid-1960s

Percent of total income or benefits

Source and year	Lower 20 percent	Lower 40 percent	Lower 60 percent	Top 40 percent	Top 20 percent	Top 5 percent	Gini concentration ratio[a]
Farmer and farm manager total money income, 1963	3.2	11.7	26.4	73.6	50.5	20.8	0.468
Program benefits							
Sugar cane, 1965	1.0	2.9	6.3	93.7	83.1	63.2	0.799
Cotton, 1964	1.8	6.6	15.1	84.9	69.2	41.2	0.653
Rice, 1963	1.0	5.5	15.1	84.9	65.3	34.6	0.632
Wheat, 1964							
Price supports	3.4	8.3	20.7	79.3	62.3	30.5	0.566
Direct payments	6.9	14.2	26.4	73.6	57.3	27.9	0.480
Total	3.3	8.1	20.4	79.6	62.4	30.5	0.569
Feed grains, 1964							
Price supports	0.5	3.2	15.3	84.7	57.3	24.4	0.588
Direct payments	4.4	16.1	31.8	68.2	46.8	20.7	0.405
Total	1.0	4.9	17.3	82.7	56.1	23.9	0.565
Peanuts, 1964	3.8	10.9	23.7	76.3	57.2	28.5	0.522
Tobacco, 1965	3.9	13.2	26.5	73.5	52.8	24.9	0.476
Sugar beets, 1965	5.0	14.3	27.0	73.0	50.5	24.4	0.456
Agricultural conservation program, 1964							
All eligibles	7.9	15.8	34.7	65.3	39.2	n.a.	0.343
Recipients	10.5	22.8	40.3	59.7	36.6	13.8	0.271

Source: James T. Bonnen, "The Absence of Knowledge of Distributional Impacts: An Obstacle to Effective Public Program Analysis and Decisions," in *The Analysis and Evaluation of Public Expenditures: The PPB System,* A Compendium of Papers Submitted to the Subcommittee on Economy in Government of the Joint Economic Committee, 91 Cong. 1 sess. (1969), Vol. I, Table 7, p. 440.

n.a. = not available.

a. The more closely the Gini concentration ratio approaches 1, the more unequal is the distribution; 0 represents a completely equal distribution.

direct payment benefits of the farm commodity programs are more highly concentrated among large farmers than is farm income itself.[2] In almost every case, the top 20 percent of farmers got more than half the benefits. Conversely, the smallest 40 percent of farmers received only a very modest fraction of the benefits, usually less than 10 percent. The difference in the degree of

2. The agricultural conservation program, which shows the least concentration, is not a commodity support program and therefore is not tied to production volume. Moreover, it has certain built-in features effectively limiting the payment large farmers can receive.

concentration of benefits among different programs (sugar, rice, wheat, and so forth) appears to depend primarily on the degree of concentration of their production and sales among larger producers. Analysis of census of agriculture data indicates that the ranking of crops by benefits concentration, as in the Bonnen table, would match a ranking by sales concentration. Production of sugar cane, cotton, and rice is far more concentrated among large producers than is production of wheat, feed grains, peanuts, tobacco, and sugar beets.

The very nature of current price support programs guarantees that benefits will be more heavily concentrated among large farmers than is total farm income. On small farms, net income is a high percentage of cash receipts. Much of the small farmer's input is his own labor, the return to which is treated not as an expense but as part of income. While large farmers' cash receipts are much higher, their expenses—for fertilizer, machinery, and hired labor—are also much greater. Their own labor is a smaller fraction of total inputs and their net income a smaller fraction of cash receipts than are those of small farmers. Price supports raise prices and cash receipts above free market levels by about the same percentage for large and small farmers, but raise net income proportionately more for large farmers than for small ones. And the large farmers' share of total price support benefits will be proportionally larger than their share of net income.

An example will help. Assume a situation with two farm classes, each with the following characteristics (remembering that the return to the farmer's own labor is included in the net income figure):

Item	Total	One large farm	Five small farms
Cash receipts	$110,000	$60,000	$50,000
Expenses	75,000	45,000	30,000
Net income	$ 35,000	$15,000	$20,000

Now assume a price support program that raises prices and cash receipts by 20 percent. The result will be as follows:

Item	Total	One large farm	Five small farms
Original cash receipts	$110,000	$60,000	$50,000
Addition from price supports (20 percent of cash receipts)	22,000	12,000	10,000
Less: expenses	75,000	45,000	30,000
Net income	$ 57,000	$27,000	$30,000
Percent of net income before price supports	100	43	57
Percent of total price support benefits	100	55	45

The Bonnen approach to measuring the distribution of benefits from farm programs has one major advantage. It does not require the very difficult and controversial estimate of the dollar value of price support benefits, which involves a calculation of what free market prices and incomes would be. Since it only seeks to determine the relative distribution of benefits, the Bonnen approach avoids the necessity of calculating absolute benefits.

But one of the shortcomings of Bonnen's measurements is their failure to provide information on the income level of the farmers receiving the benefits. A concentration of 57 percent of price support benefits among the top 20 percent of feed grain producers, ranked by size of acreage, is indeed significant. But in terms of income distribution, it makes all the difference in the world whether their net income averages $4,000 per year or $20,000. If their average income were $4,000, those producers by most standards would be judged far from affluent. The opposite judgment would seem reasonable in the $20,000 case. The income distribution effects of farm programs can best be judged by the distribution of benefits by income size class and the absolute magnitude of the income support provided each farm income group.

Even for judging the relative distribution of benefits, it is improper to assume a one-to-one correlation between acreage size class and economic size class. Not all large farms have large sales and income; and not all farms with high sales and income are large acreage farms. The 1964 census of agriculture showed, for example, that there were 19,300 feed grain farms with annual sales of over $40,000. The average size of these farms was 1,540 acres. But 2,800 of them were of less than 500 acres, and 7,000 less than 700 acres. Conversely, 106,000 feed grain farms had annual sales in the $5,000-$10,000 range, and an average size of 347 acres. Yet, 19,000 of these farms had more than 500 acres. There were almost as many farms in this $5,000-$10,000 sales class, with acreages in the 1,000 to 2,000 range, as there were in the $40,000-and-over sales class.

Another problem in distributing benefits by acreage classes is the large number of farms that produce significant amounts of more than one product. A farm with a small acreage of cotton may have a large acreage devoted to soybeans. Feed grain producers may also grow wheat, and vice versa. In 1968, for example, of the farmers who received total payments exceeding $10,000, 21,000 received cotton payments in combination with direct payments under other programs such as feed grain, wool, and wheat. Only 7,768 farmers received cotton payments exclusively. Distributing benefits by farm size group on a crop-by-crop basis does not reveal the distributive effects of multiple cropping.

Distribution of Benefits by Income Groups

Determining how the benefits from U.S. farm programs are distributed among farmers of different income levels presents three major problems: measuring the magnitude of the benefits; estimating the distribution of benefits to farms grouped according to economic class; and relating the economic class grouping to a net income grouping.

Measuring the Magnitude of the Benefits

Data are readily available on the magnitude of direct payment benefits. Table 4 summarizes those payments annually from 1955 to 1969. Except for

Table 4. Direct Payments under Various Farm Programs, 1955 through 1969
In millions of dollars

	Farm program								
Year	Conservation [a]	Soil bank	Sugar	Wool	Feed grain	Wheat	Cotton	Cropland adjustment	Total
1955	188	...	41	...	...	...	...	...	229
1956	220	243	37	54	...	...	...	...	554
1957	230	700	32	53	...	...	...	...	1,016
1958	215	815	44	14	...	...	...	...	1,089
1959	233	323	44	82	...	...	...	...	682
1960	223	370	59	51	...	...	...	...	702
1961	236	334	53	56	772	42	...	...	1,493
1962	230	304	64	54	841	253	...	...	1,747
1963	231	304	67	37	843	215	...	...	1,696
1964	236	199	79	25	1,163	438	39	...	2,181
1965	224	160	75	18	1,139	525	70	...	2,463
1966	231	145	71	34	1,293	679	773	51	3,277
1967	237	129	70	29	865	731	932	85	3,079
1968	227	114	75	66	1,366	747	787	81	3,462
1969	201	46	78	61	1,643	858	828	78	3,794

Source: USDA, Economic Research Service (ERS), *Farm Income Situation*, FIS-216 (July 1970), p. 64.

a. Includes payments under the agricultural conservation program (ACP) and the Great Plains conservation program.

a sharp peak in 1957 and 1958, as the soil bank contracts were inaugurated, payments have grown steadily over the period, from $229 million in 1955 to $3.8 billion in 1969.[3] This increase is partly due to the more ambitious

3. The total budgetary costs of farm programs exceed this amount because they include administrative expenses, storage and interest costs, inventory transactions, and similar items.

income and price support objectives adopted in the early 1960s. Beginning in 1961, direct payments were made to feed grain producers as a means of purchasing acreage restrictions. In 1963, direct payments were partially substituted for high market price supports and mandatory controls in the feed grains program, in 1964 in the wheat program, and in 1965 in the cotton program. Continued large increases in yields raised the cost of achieving supply controls for feed grains, and to a lesser extent wheat. At any given support price level, increases in yields raise the potential return on planted acres and, therefore, the cost of inducing farmers to forgo planting.

Farm income exclusive of direct payments has remained remarkably constant since the late 1950s. The continuing rise in total farm income is therefore due to the steady increase in direct payments (see Table 5).[4] Total income per farm has risen even more sharply.

Table 5. Net Farm Income, with and without Direct Payments, 1955 through 1969

Period	Realized net income, excluding payments	Direct payments[a]	Realized net income, including payments
	Average annual total income (millions of dollars)		
1956-60	11,666	10	11,676
1961-65	11,755	1,230	12,985
1966-69	12,774	2,660	15,434
1967-69[b]	12,430	2,704	15,134
	Average annual income per farm (dollars)		
1956-60	2,761	2	2,763
1961-65	3,307	345	3,652
1966-69	4,123	857	4,980
1967-69[b]	4,074	885	4,959

Source: *Farm Income Situation,* July 1970, pp. 44, 46, 57, 64.

a. Direct payments for wheat (including value of certificates paid by processors), feed grains, cotton, sugar, and wool; excludes portion going to nonfarm landlords.

b. These figures show the final period excluding 1966, a year of exceptionally short crops and high income.

Price support benefits are, of course, much more difficult to estimate than direct payment benefits, since they represent the difference between income actually earned by farmers in the sale of farm products and the income they

4. This is not to say that income per farm, exclusive of direct payments, would have remained constant had farm programs been abolished and direct payments been eliminated. Because they were used in part to purchase reductions in farm output, direct payments helped keep farm prices and cash receipts from marketings at higher levels than would otherwise have prevailed.

would have earned under free market conditions. Without supply controls, production of most, if not all, price-supported crops would increase. Prices would fall, and with low price elasticities of demand, cash receipts of farmers would be reduced. The prices, output, and incomes that would prevail under these conditions must be estimated in order to measure price support benefits. The wide range of factors, about which some estimates must be made, includes:

1. Acreages planted and yields of various crops with acreage restrictions removed and CCC loans and purchases eliminated;

2. The price elasticities of demand, both domestic and export, for the commodities involved;

3. The impact of lower grain prices on livestock feeding, production, and sales;

4. The impact of lower returns from previously price-supported crops on the production and prices of other commodities. Because of the substitutability, both in production and consumption, among farm commodities, the effect of removing price supports would extend to returns from other commodities as well as from price-supported crops;

5. The changes in production expenses that would occur under free market conditions. On the one hand, increased output would tend to raise expenses. On the other hand, several factors would tend to reduce them: prices for purchased feed, seed, and livestock would be lower; removal of the acreage restrictions that are currently used to control supplies would improve the mix of inputs (land, labor, capital) and thereby lead toward lower costs; with sharply lower incomes, farmers' ability to purchase machinery and other capital would be curtailed.

In the short run the major impact of the removal of price supports would fall directly on the price-supported crops. After some period of time, livestock prices and cash receipts would drop as lower grain prices stimulated additional meat production. Also, the lower returns from planting the previously price-supported crops would induce larger production and lower prices for other crops. Even those relatively efficient farmers who today produce the bulk of farm output and earn returns on their investment and labor equivalent to what they would realize in nonfarm employment would, for some time at least, earn subnormal returns.

Over a longer period of time the reduced returns from producing farm commodities should lead to some restrictions of supply and to a partial recovery of prices. While the larger farmers who produce most of agricultural output might not cut back their production, many marginal farmers would in the long run be forced out of farming altogether. The exodus from farming would be accelerated (unless unemployment rates outside of farming were high). Prices would rise more nearly to cover costs, including a reasonable return on investment and family labor for those who produced the bulk of farm output. Whether farming would eventually become as economically attractive as other sectors of the economy, and how long it would take for subnormal farm returns to be eliminated, is a matter about which there is much controversy and little knowledge. In any event, current farm programs are primarily designed precisely to avoid this long period of subnormal returns to large farmers.

The estimates of free market prices and incomes used in calculating price support benefits do not take into account the long-term adjustment. They cover a period long enough to allow the impact on livestock production and non-price-supported crops to occur, but not long enough to allow for an accelerated exodus of farmers to other occupations. As a consequence the measure of price support benefits used here—however accurately it may portray the short- and intermediate-run effects of current farm programs—does overstate the long-run supplement to farmers' income these programs provide.

Free Market Estimates of Farm Prices and Incomes

In the early 1960s a number of pioneering efforts were undertaken to construct models of the farm economy that could be used to predict farm prices, output, and income under varying conditions. Some of these models were designed in response to congressional requests for estimates of the consequences of various alternative farm programs, including one without price supports or supply controls.

The Joint Economic Committee of the Congress in 1960 published the results of a model, constructed by George Brandow of Pennsylvania State University, that projected farm prices, output, and incomes to 1965 under the assumption that price supports and supply controls had been eliminated. Another model, developed by the U.S. Department of Agriculture to make the same projections under roughly corresponding assumptions, was also published in 1960 by the Senate Agriculture and Forestry Committee as Senate Document 77. Periodically since then, the Economic Research Service (ERS) of the Department of Agriculture has used a model of the farm economy to estimate the impact of removing price support and supply control programs; the results have been summarized in various congressional publications. The 1968 ERS model estimates what the major farm economic variables would have been under free market conditions during the period 1961 to 1967. In 1968 Professors Mayer, Heady, and Madsen of Iowa State University's Center for Agricultural and Economic Development (CAED) projected farm prices, output, and incomes to 1970 under alternative farm programs, including a free market set of conditions. Unlike the other models, the CAED model included a projection of the long-term consequence of removing farm programs, allowing for an accelerated exodus from farming. Essentially, this projection estimated the balance between free market demand and supply on the assumption that marginal farms would be abandoned to the point where prices rose to cover the costs of production, including an imputed return to family and hired labor and to investment in farm capital.

Table 6 shows, for the relevant period covered by each of the four models, the difference between actual farm income and farm income under free market conditions. The Senate and JEC models projected free market conditions in

Table 6. Projected Decline in Realized Net Farm Income and Major Government Payments with Removal of Major Price Support Programs
In billions of dollars

Income comparison	*Decline in income, excluding payments*	*Decline in government payments*[a]	*Decline in income, including payments*
Senate model[b]			
1965 free market/actual 1959	4.4	0	4.4
1965 free market/actual 1965	5.2	1.8	7.0
JEC model[c]			
1965 free market/actual 1959	4.2	0	4.2
1965 free market/actual 1965	5.0	1.8	6.8
ERS model[d]			
1961-67 free market/actual 1961-67	3.3	1.7	5.0
1965-67 free market/actual 1965-67	3.4	2.5	5.9
CAED model[e]			
Short run: free market/actual	3.0	2.9	5.9
Long run: free market/actual	1.4	2.9	4.3

a. Direct payments under the wheat, cotton, and feed grain programs (including wheat certificates purchased by processors).

b. *Report from the United States Department of Agriculture and a Statement from the Land Grant Colleges IRM-1, Advisory Committee on Farm Price and Income Projections, 1960-65, Under Conditions Approximating Free Production and Marketing of Agricultural Commodities,* S. Doc. 77, 86 Cong. 2 sess. (1960). Price support programs were assumed to have been removed by 1960.

c. *Economic Policies for Agriculture in the 1960's: Implications of Four Selected Alternatives,* prepared for the Joint Economic Committee, 86 Cong. 2 sess. (1960), Part I and App. A. Price support programs were assumed to have been removed by 1960.

d. *Farm Program and Farm Bargaining,* Hearings before the Senate Committee on Agriculture and Forestry, 90 Cong. 2 sess. (1968), pp. 588-90. Price support programs were assumed to have been removed prior to the 1961 crop.

e. Leo V. Mayer and others, *Farm Programs for the 1970's,* CAED Report 32 (Iowa State University, Center for Agricultural and Economic Development, 1968).

1965.[5] Their comparisons of actual 1959 farm income and 1965 free market income are obviously an understatement of price support benefits in 1965, since they do not take account of the substantial rise in the level of supports between 1959 and 1965. Their comparisons of actual income in 1965 and free market income in 1965 reflect not only the models' predictions of the effect of dropping price supports but also any other variations between the assumed and actual conditions in 1965.

The ERS model does not run afoul of this problem. Its comparison of actual with free market conditions during the 1961-67 period, made in 1968, was based on known conditions. Free market income differs from actual income only because of the removal of price supports; the ERS model contains only the imperfections attendant on estimating the impact of removing price supports and not the additional disturbances that may be reflected in the other comparisons.

Despite the potential differences, the results of the three models are not markedly different. The ERS model assumes that price supports were removed after the 1960 crop season, so that by the 1965-67 period the prices of livestock and non-price-supported crops would have been affected. Farm income was estimated to be $6 billion lower under free market conditions. According to the Senate and JEC models, which assumed the removal of price supports after the 1959 crop season, farm income would have dropped $7 billion. The actual figures used in the ERS model show that the larger part of the income decline was due to the cessation of direct payments and the smaller part to price support actions. The other two models do not reflect the fact that direct payments grew steadily during these years and averaged a good bit higher during the 1965-67 period than they did in the year 1965 itself.

The CAED model shows, for the short run, the same total impact of eliminating commodity programs as does the ERS model. The long-run CAED model is not comparable with the others, however, since it assumes a major withdrawal of resources out of agriculture.[6]

The distribution estimates in this study rely upon the ERS model's estimates of price support benefits. At least for the period during which there is

5. In both models, land retired under the soil bank was assumed to be 30 million acres. Land retirements obviously do support prices. Hence the full impact of free market prices was not shown.
6. Actually, the CAED model even in the short run differs from the ERS 1965-67 model significantly, even though the total $5.9 billion income decline is the same in the two models. The CAED short-run model refers to the first year after the elimination of major price support programs and hence does not allow for significant repercussions in markets for non-price-supported commodities. Its $5.9 billion reduction is concentrated almost wholly in price-supported commodities.

not a significant acceleration of the exodus from farming, the results of the model are roughly consistent with estimates made by other investigators.

The ERS model defined the free market as one in which price supports, supply controls, and direct payments were eliminated on all major farm commodities. However, sugar and wool subsidy payments were assumed to have continued, as were payments under the agricultural conservation program. Government-assisted exports of agricultural commodities under Public Law 480 were also assumed to have remained at the actual levels of the period. In this study, Public Law 480 shipments are assumed to remain unchanged. But sugar, wool, and ACP direct payments are assumed to have been eliminated. The marketing allotments and import quotas currently supporting domestic sugar cane and beet prices are eliminated, so that domestic sugar prices reflect world price levels during the period in question. For the 1965-67 period these additional assumptions would change the estimated ERS value of price support benefits from $3.4 billion to $3.5 billion (on account of removing the support from sugar prices) and the direct payment benefits from $2.5 billion to $3 billion (reflecting the value of the direct sugar, wool, and ACP subsidies).

Distribution of Benefits by Economic Class

The Department of Agriculture classifies farms into the following categories, according to the value of their sales receipts: [7]

Economic class	Value of sales (thousands of dollars)	Percent of total farm sales, 1969	Percent of total number of farms, 1969
I	40 and over	51.3	7.1
II	20-40	21.3	12.0
III	10-20	16.0	17.0
IV	5-10	6.3	13.1
V	2.5-5	2.4	9.6
VI	Less than 2.5	2.7	41.2

For 1964, extensive census data are available on various characteristics of farms grouped by economic class, including data on production and sales of each major commodity by farms in each economic class. The distribution of benefits in 1964 was estimated from these data. The 1964 distributions were

7. USDA, ERS, *Farm Income Situation*, FIS-216 (July 1970), pp. 68, 71. Class VI includes a number of categories that the Bureau of the Census shows separately (small commercial farms, part-time farms, and so forth); with one very minor exception these categories all have the common characteristic of selling less than $2,500 of farm products each year.

then applied to the Department of Agriculture's 1969 estimates of cash receipts, production expenses, and net income for each economic class to produce an estimate of the distribution of farm program benefits by economic class for 1969. Quite different approaches were used to distribute price support benefits and direct payment benefits.

Price Support Benefits. Price support benefits, reflecting the support of market prices afforded by farm commodity programs, were estimated from the data underlying the ERS model. For each major commodity group—wheat, feed grains, cotton, livestock, and all other commodities—estimates were made of the decline in net income that would have occurred during the 1961-67 period had price supports and acreage restrictions been removed. The loss was first distributed to each of the six economic classes of farms in proportion to its share in the production of that commodity group, according to the 1964 census data. The losses in the various commodities were then summed to give an estimate of total losses within each of the economic classes. In effect, the ERS model provided a rough measure of price support benefits for the 1961-67 period as a whole, and the 1964 census determined the distribution of those benefits by economic class. The resulting distribution of price support benefits is very similar to a simple distribution of cash receipts (excluding direct payments) for 1964, as the following percentages received by the various economic classes show: [8]

		Economic class				
Distribution	*I*	*II*	*III*	*IV*	*V*	*VI*
Price support benefits	42.3	19.3	17.9	11.0	5.3	4.2
Cash receipts	40.7	20.0	19.0	10.9	4.9	4.5

The close similarity in the distributions of price support benefits and cash receipts is not surprising. The two distributions can be obtained by weighting the basic production distributions for individual commodities by their shares in total price support benefits on the one hand, and total cash receipts on the other. The similarity of the aggregate distributions implies that, if the secondary effects on non-price-supported crops are taken into account, the aggregate distributions by economic class ought not to differ from each other. Thus it seems reasonable to use the aggregate distribution of cash receipts to approximate the aggregate distribution of price support benefits for 1969, a year for which no census data are available on individual crop distributions by economic class.

8. Price support benefits are from Appendix B, Table B-1; cash receipts are from *Farm Income Situation,* July 1970, p. 71.

Direct Payment Benefits. A follow-up sample survey conducted by the Department of Agriculture in 1965 to augment the 1964 census data included information on the volume of direct government payments received by farmers in each economic class. This information is used as the basis for distributing direct payments. The data are by no means perfect. In particular, the total volume of direct payments received, as estimated from the sample responses in the 1965 survey ($1.6 billion), fell significantly short of the total payment outlays recorded on government books ($2.2 billion). There was, clearly, substantial under-reporting. The discrepancy may arise from the fact that the census reported only payments received by farm operators; some unknown amount goes to nonfarm landlords. Although there is no way of knowing whether under-reporting varied by economic class, the distribution of direct payments based on the survey data appears to be consistent with other information about direct payment programs (see Appendix A); hence the survey data, with minor modifications, are used in the analysis.[9]

Total Benefits from Farm Programs, 1964

Table 7 presents the information on direct payments and combines it with the distribution of price support benefits to reach a distribution of total benefits from farm programs in 1964. The total benefits per farm are then compared to the average net income of farmers in each economic class.

Benefit Distribution, 1969

The basic distributions of price support and direct payment benefits for 1969 were made by using the 1964 data in a variety of ways.

Price Support Benefits

Since in 1964 the distribution of cash receipts (excluding government payments) reasonably well approximated the distribution of price support benefits, the cash receipts data were used to estimate the distribution of benefits in 1969. The aggregate value of price support benefits again represented the average difference, from the ERS model, between actual and free market farm income (exclusive of direct payments) for the years 1965-67. (No estimate

9. In 1964 there was a small amount of direct cotton payments. These were distributed in accordance with cotton production and added to the 1965 survey distribution.

Table 7. Distribution of Farm Program Benefits and Income by Economic Class, 1964

Item	I	II	III	IV	V	VI	I & II	V & VI
				Economic class				
Aggregate benefits				*(billions of dollars)*				
Price supports	1.44	0.66	0.61	0.37	0.18	0.14	2.09	0.32
Direct payments	0.34	0.44	0.58	0.38	0.19	0.26	0.78	0.45
Total	1.78	1.10	1.19	0.75	0.37	0.40	2.87	0.77
Distribution of benefits				*(percent of total)*				
Price supports	42.3	19.3	17.9	11.0	5.3	4.2	61.6	9.5
Direct payments	15.4	20.3	26.4	17.4	8.6	12.0	35.7	20.6
Total	31.8	19.7	21.3	13.4	6.6	7.2	51.3	13.8
Income and benefits per farm				*(thousands of dollars)*				
Farmer's net income	27.3	11.8	8.0	6.3	5.0	5.1	17.3	5.1
Net income from farming	23.3	9.5	6.0	3.5	2.0	1.0	14.4	1.2
Price supports	9.9	2.5	1.3	0.7	0.4	0.1	5.0	0.2
Direct payments	2.3	1.6	1.2	0.7	0.4	0.2	1.9	0.2
Total	12.2	4.1	2.5	1.4	0.8	0.3	6.9	0.4
Net income from farming under free market conditions	11.1	5.4	3.5	2.1	1.2	0.7	7.5	0.8

Source: Appendix B, Table B-1, and *Farm Income Situation,* July 1970.

was available for the years beyond 1967.) If the ratio of benefits to cash receipts were assumed to have remained unchanged from 1966-67 to 1969, then because cash receipts increased over the period, the aggregate value of price support benefits would also have increased—from $3.6 billion to $4.5 billion. If the ratio in the single year 1967 were used, the value of benefits in 1969 would have been even larger, $4.7 billion. In the case of some major crops (particularly cotton), however, prices were closer to free market levels in 1969 than in the 1965-67 period. In view of this fact, and in an attempt to present conservative estimates, the 1969 estimate of $3.6 billion is used, implying a decline in the ratio of price support benefits to cash receipts over the period.

Direct Payments

The distribution of direct payments in 1969 under the cotton program was calculated separately from that for other programs. The voluntary diversion program for cotton was started in 1965, one year later than the period to which the sample survey data on direct payments refer. Since cotton production is much more highly concentrated among large farmers than is the production of wheat and feed grains, which dominated the 1964 census, the sample survey substantially understates the concentration of total direct payments in years after 1964. In order to estimate their distribution, 1969 cotton payments were assumed to be proportional to the distribution of cotton production in 1964. This method of distribution has two biases that, fortunately, run in opposite directions. On the one hand, farmers with less than 10 acres receive certain special benefits under the program, so that a production distribution tends to overstate the concentration of benefits among large farmers. On the other hand, the economic class boundaries are fixed in dollar terms; for example, Class I includes sales of $40,000 and over. Over time the average size and cash receipts of farms tend to grow—some farmers move up from one class to another, and those who leave farming tend to be principally in the lower economic classes. Hence a 1964 distribution understates the percentage of cotton production taking place in the top economic classes and overstates the percentage accounted for by the lower economic classes. Because the quantitative impact of the opposing biases may not be the same, the 1969 distribution of cotton payments by economic class must remain mildly suspect.

The distribution of direct payments for all other programs was determined from the ratio of direct payments (excluding cotton) to cash receipts in 1964 for each economic class. That ratio was applied to 1969 cash receipts, and the resulting figures were used to distribute the 1969 direct payments.

The results of both calculations are shown in Table 8. In 1969 Class I farms accounted for 7.1 percent of all farms. But they received 40.3 percent of the benefits from farm commodity programs. Average net income of these farm operators (from both farm and nonfarm sources) was $33,000, of which 42 percent, or $14,000 per farm, could be attributed to farm commodity programs. Class I and II farms taken together represented only 19.1 percent of all farms but received 62.8 percent of total benefits. Farm commodity programs contributed $8,000 of their $21,000 average net income.

At the other end of the scale Class V and VI farms accounted for 50.8 percent of total farms, but received only 9.1 percent of the subsidy benefits. The average net benefit per farm was only $400, about 5 percent of their average net income from farm and nonfarm sources.

The proportion of benefits received by large-scale farms rose between 1964 and 1969 (compare Tables 7 and 8). This change reflects in part the steady trend toward larger farms; the proportion of total production and cash receipts accounted for by Class I and Class II farms continued to rise. The concentration of direct payments also increased because the benefits of the cotton price

Table 8. Distribution of Farm Program Benefits and Income by Economic Class, 1969

| | Economic class | | | | | | | |
Item	I	II	III	IV	V	VI	I & II	V & VI
Aggregate benefits	*(billions of dollars)*							
Price supports	1.90	0.76	0.55	0.22	0.08	0.09	2.66	0.17
Direct payments	1.08	0.90	0.88	0.43	0.20	0.30	1.98	0.50
Total	2.98	1.66	1.43	0.65	0.28	0.39	4.64	0.67
Distribution of benefits	*(percent of total)*							
Price supports	52.9	21.0	15.4	6.1	2.2	2.4	73.9	4.6
Direct payments	28.5	23.7	23.2	11.3	5.3	7.9	53.6	13.2
Total	40.3	22.5	19.4	8.8	3.8	5.3	62.8	9.1
Income and benefits per farm	*(thousands of dollars)*							
Farmer's net income	33.0	13.7	9.6	8.1	7.0	8.1	20.9	7.9
Net income from farming	27.5	10.5	6.5	3.6	2.1	1.1	16.8	1.3
Price supports	9.0	2.1	1.1	0.6	0.3	0.1	4.7	0.1
Direct payments	5.1	2.5	1.7	1.1	0.7	0.2	3.6	0.3
Total	14.1	4.6	2.8	1.7	1.0	0.3	8.3	0.4
Net income from farming under free market conditions	13.4	5.9	3.7	1.9	1.1	0.8	8.5	0.9

Source: Appendix B, Table B-1, and *Farm Income Situation*, July 1970.

support program enacted in 1965 were heavily concentrated among large producers.

By their very nature, current farm programs tend to provide benefits—paid for by both consumers and taxpayers—primarily to those larger farmers who produce the bulk of agricultural output. Conversely, the very large number of small farmers, who in the aggregate produce only a modest fraction of total farm output, are helped relatively little by these programs.

CHAPTER FOUR

FARM SUBSIDIES
AND FARMLAND PRICES

As pointed out earlier, farm subsidies are vested not in the farmer as an individual but in the process of farming itself. Returns from farming are raised above the level that would prevail in the absence of farm programs. In most circumstances the increased returns tend to be translated into higher land prices.

The net income a farmer receives from his farm operation is itself a combination of several elements. It includes a return on his equity investment in machinery, equipment, and buildings. It also includes a return on the unpaid labor he and his family contribute to the farm. The remainder is the return he receives for his equity investment in land—an imputed net rent on farmland. The price of land for farm use will, therefore, depend upon how much farmers are willing to pay to secure this net rent. The ratio between the price of farm land and its annual net rent is the capitalization ratio. If a piece of land that is expected to yield $10,000 per year in net rent is sold at $200,000, then the capitalization ratio is 20 to 1. In this case the farmer is willing to pay a price reflecting a 5 percent per year return on his investment.

The value of net rent itself depends upon the returns farmers are willing to accept for their own labor and their investment in machinery and buildings. Assume, for example, a farming operation that is expected to yield an annual net income, after all expenses, of $25,000 per year, with an investment of $100,000 in machinery and buildings necessary to secure that income. Assume also that the farmer demands an expectation of a 5 percent return on his capital before he is willing to invest funds in the operation. If the farmer pays $240,000 for the land, he presumably values his own (and his family's) labor at $8,000 per year and he considers the land to yield him a net rent of $12,000. (A 5 percent return on his $100,000 investment in machinery and buildings is $5,000 per year; add to this the $8,000 for his labor; the remaining income is $12,000 per year in net rent, which at a land price of $240,000 represents a 5 percent rate of return.)

Figure 1. Indices of Land Value and Farm Income per Acre, 1935-36 through 1965-67

Index: 1935-39 = 100

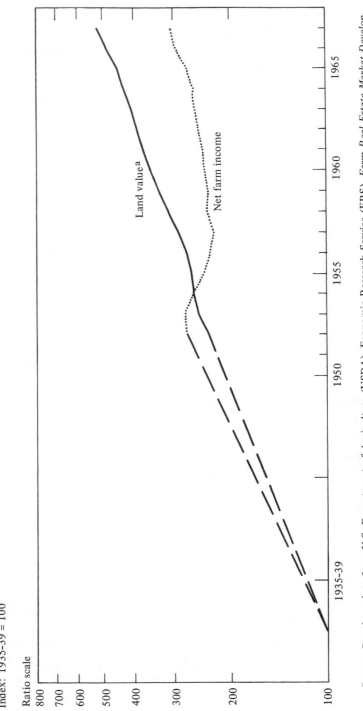

Source: Based on data from U.S. Department of Agriculture (USDA), Economic Research Service (ERS), *Farm Real Estate Market Development*, various issues; USDA, ERS, *Farm Income Situation*, FIS-216 (July 1970), p. 44; and USDA, *Agricultural Statistics*, various issues.
a. Includes value of service buildings.

So long as the rate of return farmers require as the condition of investing in machinery and equipment remains unchanged, and there is no change in the wage rate they expect on their own labor, then any increase in the return from farming brought about by higher commodity prices will be considered an addition to the net rent of land. In turn, so long as the capitalization ratio remains unchanged—that is, so long as the rate of return farmers require as the condition for investing in land does not change—the price of land will rise in proportion to the increase in net rent. Land prices will be bid up as farmers seek to secure the higher net rent.

Growth in Farmland Prices

A comparison of the trend in farm income with the trend in agricultural land prices would appear to refute this contention. Farmland prices have risen much more sharply than has farm income, as the following percentage increases per acre over the past thirty years show: [1]

Period	Increase in net farm income	Increase in value of land
1935-39 to 1952-54	160	160
1952-54 to 1965-67	18	100
1935-39 to 1965-67	206	420

While the percentage rise in farmland prices per acre was just about equal to the percentage rise in farm income per acre between 1935-39 and 1952-54, land prices rose very steeply in subsequent years, while income did not. Over the entire period from 1935-39 to 1965-67, the percentage increase in income was less than half the gain in land prices. These relative changes are illustrated in Figure 1.

The excessive growth in land prices relative to farm income has led to some speculation that the nonfarm demand for land on the fringes of rapidly growing urban areas has driven up the price of farmland beyond its value in farming. In fact, however, the rise in farmland prices over the past thirty years can be well explained by what has happened to the net rent of farmland in farm uses.

Net rent to farmland is not the same as net farm income. On the one hand, farm income includes returns to factors other than land. On the other hand,

---

1. Based on data in USDA, ERS, *Farm Real Estate Market Developments,* various issues; *Farm Income Situation,* various issues; and *Census of Agriculture, 1964,* Vol. 2, Chap. 3: *Size of Farm* (1967), p. 241. The land price data include the value of farm service buildings; however, such buildings are a modest fraction of the total, and their inclusion does not significantly distort the figures.

Figure 2. Indices of Land Value, Farm Income, and Land Rent per Acre, 1935-39 through 1965-67

Index: 1935-39 = 100

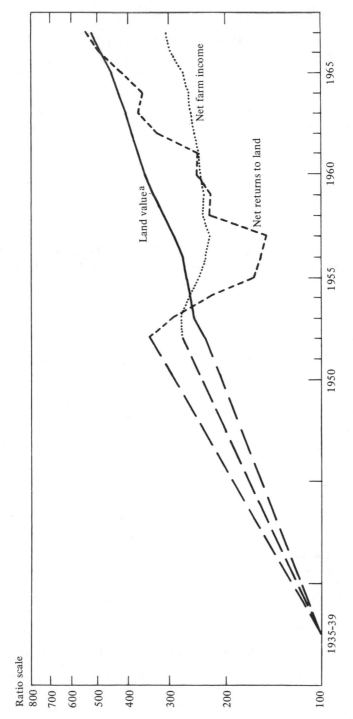

Source: Same as Figure 1.
a. Includes value of service buildings.

some of the net rent to farmland does not enter farm income but is siphoned off as cash rent paid to nonfarm landlords and as interest payments on farm real estate mortgage debt.

Bruce Johnson of the Economic Research Service of the Department of Agriculture has estimated the net returns to land in agriculture.[2] The return to land, using his approach with some modifications, can be calculated as: net farm income *plus* interest on farm real estate debt *plus* net rent to nonfarm landlords *minus* imputed returns to farm operator and family labor *minus* imputed return to equity investment in non-real-estate capital *minus* net rental value of dwellings *minus* imputed charge for management. In effect this technique estimates the return to land as a residual, after imputing a return to farm family labor and investment in non-real-estate capital.

If the increases in land prices and farm income are compared to increases in the net return to land, the long-term growth of land prices is no longer surprising. The percentage increases per acre for the three factors are as follows: [3]

Period	Increase in net farm income	Increase in net return to land	Increase in value of land
1935-39 to 1952-54	160	124	160
1952-54 to 1965-67	18	143	100
1935-39 to 1965-67	206	444	420

Over the past thirty years as a whole, land prices have risen by very close to the same percentage as net returns to land. Over this period, net returns to land have fluctuated more sharply, but have risen much more rapidly than farm income. Figure 2 illustrates these changes.

The rising net returns to farmland have been capitalized into higher land prices. As land was gradually turned over at higher prices, the carrying costs of the higher-priced land, together with rising interest rates, siphoned off a significant part of the gain from farm income. Rents paid to nonfarm landlords also rose substantially.

Returns to land are a residual income. As farm income in the middle 1950s fell sharply from the Korean War peaks, returns to land fell even more drastically. But with the effective introduction of high price support levels in the 1960s, returns to land began to rise rapidly, and the ratio of land returns to

2. Bruce B. Johnson, "An Active Land Market in Perspective," *Farm Real Estate Market Developments*, CD-71 (December 1968), pp. 27-35.

3. Based on data in *Farm Real Estate Market Developments*, various issues; *Farm Income Situation*, various issues; and *Size of Farm*, p. 241. The land price data include the value of farm service buildings; however, such buildings are a modest fraction of the total, and their inclusion does not significantly distort the figures.

Table 9. Ratio of Net Land Returns to Net Farm Income, 1935-39 and 1952 through 1967[a]

Year	Ratio	Year	Ratio
1935-39	0.249	1960	0.253
1952	0.318	1961	0.250
1953	0.262	1962	0.322
1954	0.214	1963	0.362
1955	0.167	1964	0.347
1956	0.168	1965	0.386
1957	0.167	1966	0.416
1958	0.239	1967	0.442
1959	0.238		

Source: Based on data from USDA, ERS, *Farm Real Estate Market Developments,* various issues; *Farm Income Situation,* various issues; and *Size of Farm.*
a. To avoid erratic year-to-year fluctuations, all data except for 1935-39 are expressed in three-year moving averages centered in the last year.

net farm income increased markedly (see Table 9). By 1967 net returns to land were equal to 44 percent of farm income, almost double the prewar relationship.

Ratio of Land Returns to Income

The threefold combination of farm price supports, rapidly advancing technology, and the capitalization process that determines land prices inevitably tends to raise the ratio of land returns to net farm income. The joint influence of price supports and rapidly advancing technology has been described by Herdt and Cochrane.[4] As individual farmers adopt new technology—higher yielding seed strains, better fertilizers, new types of machinery—average unit costs are reduced. At existing prices, the profitability of farm operations rises. So long as price support programs maintain prices, farmers will have an incentive to expand output, in the short run by increasing variable inputs (such as fertilizer and pesticides), and in the long run by purchasing additional land. Or to say this another way, the net rent of land will be increased by the maintenance of prices in the face of lower unit costs brought about by new technology, as a consequence of which land prices will rise as farmers seek to expand their holdings. Even though the total acreage planted to many crops is restricted by governmental supply control programs, continued technological progress combined with price supports provides incentives for individual

4. Robert W. Herdt and Willard W. Cochrane, "Farm Land Prices and Farm Technological Advance," *Journal of Farm Economics,* Vol. 48 (May 1966), pp. 243-63.

farmers to purchase land in order to enlarge their own operations. Throughout the 1960s, voluntary farm real estate sales[5] each year amounted to about 30 per 1,000 farms—that is, about 3 percent of farms were sold in whole or in part each year. Each year since 1955, about two-thirds of all purchases of farmland have been made by farmers. Purchases for purposes of farm enlargement accounted for 45 percent of all purchases in 1960 and rose steadily to 57 percent of all purchases in 1968. Farm enlargement through rental of additional land has also become quite prevalent.

The simple maintenance of price supports in the presence of rapid technological advance will, therefore, tend to drive up net rent to land and paradoxically increase the demand for farmland at a time when there is an overall excess of agricultural capacity.[6] If, in addition, the level of price supports is not merely maintained but raised, as it was in the early 1960s, the rise in net rent and land prices will be even greater. In the seven years between 1958-60 and 1965-67, net returns to farmland per acre more than doubled.

The price of farmland for farm use has been influenced by several other major factors. Federal farm programs have sought to control the supply of agricultural commodities through acreage restrictions of one form or another. Other things being equal, a farmer with large acreage should be able to reduce his planted acreage more efficiently—that is, with less loss of production—than a small farmer. If acreage must be reduced by 20 percent, the choice of acres to reduce can be more efficiently made on a single 200 acre farm than on the same land split into two 100 acre farms. The incentive to buy land in order to maximize the selection of acreage to retire probably becomes minimal for farms that are already very large in scale. Under acreage control programs, however, the marginal value of additional acres to most prospective farm buyers may be at least modestly higher than the capitalized net rent of the land to the prospective seller. In effect, acreage control programs create economies of scale related not to technical factors but to the efficiency with which acres can be selected for land retirement purposes.

The rise in farmland values in recent years may also have been aided by a growing conviction among farmers that high price supports were here to stay. After the Korean War, farm returns fell sharply. At about that time a major congressional debate about farm price support programs took place, and as a result, the concept of flexible price supports was at least partially adopted. In

5. Voluntary sales are distinguished from foreclosures, estate executors' sales, and so forth.
6. Even if the new technology is very land saving, so long as prices are maintained at earlier levels, there will be an increase in the demand for land by individual producers.

the early 1960s, however, a continuing policy of high price supports was put into effect. Presumably it took some time for potential land buyers to become convinced that the increased land rents were backed by a long-term government commitment. Since the price of land depends not only on the expected future value of land rent but also upon the certainty with which those expectations are held, the process of transforming the higher rents into higher land prices took place gradually, as uncertainty diminished.

Working in the opposite direction has been the rise in interest rates during the postwar period. Interest rates measure both the carrying costs of land ownership and, roughly, the opportunity costs of equity investment in land. As interest rates rise, the capitalization ratio should fall. Other things being equal, then, an increase in interest rates should depress the price of farmland relative to its rent.

In recent years, however, the rise in interest rates has been particularly affected by expectations of continued inflation. If prices are expected to rise at, say, 3 percent per year, then an 8 percent nominal interest rate is equivalent to a 5 percent real interest rate—that is, the interest return calculated in dollars of constant purchasing power. Real interest rates have risen much less than nominal rates, undoubtedly reflecting an increase in the generally expected rate of inflation. If farmers expect that the combination of market forces and price support policies will keep farm prices more or less in line with prices generally, then the appropriate interest rate to use in determining the capitalization ratio is the real rate of interest, not the nominal rate.[7]

7. Assume that farmers expect prices of both farm inputs and farm outputs to rise at roughly the same rate as the general price index. There are, then, two equivalent ways of looking at the capitalization process. Let: L = price of land; R = expected annual net returns to land, not adjusted for expected inflation; i = nominal interest rate; i' = real interest rate; and p = expected annual increase in prices.

(1) The money value of the expected stream of net returns would be inflated by the expected rise in farm prices (which, by assumption, equals the expected rise in the general price index). This inflated stream of expected returns would be converted to a present value by a discount rate based on the nominal interest rate. Hence,

$$L = R \cdot \sum_{t=1}^{\infty} \left[\frac{1+p}{1+i} \right]^t = R \left[\frac{1}{\frac{1+i}{1+p} - 1} \right]$$

(2) The expected stream of net returns would not be inflated by the expected rise in prices, but the capitalization ratio would be the reciprocal of the real, rather than the nominal, interest rate. Hence,

$$L = R \left[\frac{1}{i'} \right] = R \left[\frac{1}{\frac{1+i}{1+p} - 1} \right]$$

Over the past thirty years as a whole, the rise in farmland prices has been roughly proportional to the rise in net rents (or returns) from farmland. The use of acreage restrictions, however, tends to raise the marginal yield of additional land to the potential purchaser above its average rent yield to the potential seller, and the continued existence of high price support policies has reduced uncertainty about future net rents. But counteracting these forces has been the rise in interest rates. On balance, it appears that the two sets of forces have been roughly offsetting.

Although price supports, combined with the advance of technology, raise the net rent of farmland, they do not similarly increase the net income of farmers. As Figure 2 and Table 9 clearly show, farmland rents have risen far more rapidly than farm income, over the past thirty years as a whole. Most of this excess gain has taken place since the late 1950s. Just before the large increase in price supports initiated in 1961, the indices of land rent and farm income (1935-39 = 100) were about equal—both had advanced by about the same percentage relative to prewar levels. In the next six years (1959-61 to 1965-67), however, land rent rose by 124 percent, while farm income rose by only 27 percent. The ratio of land rent to net farm income increased from 0.25 in 1959-61 to 0.44 in 1965-67.

Capitalization of Price Support Benefits

Because the increase in land rents brought about by price support programs is capitalized into higher land prices, many of the benefits of the farm price support programs are not felt in farm income itself, as farmland gradually changes hands (at about 3 percent per year) and as farm landlords raise cash rents to their tenant farmers. The first generation owners capture the benefits in the form of capital gains when they sell. Second generation owners lose many of the benefits to higher carrying charges. Looked at another way, a large part of the benefits of price support programs are gradually realized as capital gains upon sale of farmland, so that over time net farm income less and less reflects the benefits of farm programs. Equally as disturbing is the fact that as price support benefits are translated into higher land prices, they necessarily become frozen into farmers' asset positions. A removal or reduction in price supports would cause substantial capital losses to second generation landowners who purchased land at the higher prices and typically are paying sizable carrying costs in the form of mortgage interest. Such farmers will be worse off after the removal of farm subsidies than they would have been if the subsidies had never been introduced at all.

Viewed in this light, the concept of parity income as a possible goal for agricultural policy becomes a dubious objective. Parity income would provide the farmer a return on his own labor and investment (including investment in land) equal to what he could earn in nonfarm occupations. Price support programs are presumably needed to attain this objective because, under free market conditions, too many farmers would remain in agriculture, creating a condition of excess production and depressed incomes. But this is equivalent to saying that too many farmers will accept a less-than-parity return on their own labor (and possibly on their equity investment) while still remaining in agricultural production. If this is true, then any attempt to increase income above that level by price support programs will result in a rise in land rents, which will gradually be capitalized into higher land prices. In turn, with higher land prices, a subsequent calculation of parity income will show that price support programs have not improved the relationship between actual and parity income, since the parity rate of return, applied to the higher land prices, raises the level of parity income right along with the rise in actual income.

Subsidies, the rights to which are salable, or which are attached to salable assets as farm program subsidies are attached to land, must eventually be dissipated in the form of capital gains to asset holders. The process may take time. The asset prices may only imperfectly reflect current subsidy values, because potential purchasers may be uncertain about whether the subsidy will continue. But, at least in rough measure, such subsidies will tend to benefit primarily those who held the asset when the subsidy was introduced or increased. In the long run, farm subsidy programs, related as they are to the production of farm commodities, tend to benefit farmers chiefly in their role as landowners and not in their role as farm operators. Only as subsidies are granted to individuals, and not to salable business enterprises as such, will the benefits of the subsidy escape capitalization into higher asset prices.

Transfer Costs and National Income Costs
of Farm Subsidy Programs

Two quite different kinds of costs are associated with the farm price support programs. Transfer costs represent the amounts the nonfarm sector of the economy transfers to the farm sector. These costs are themselves of two kinds: taxpayers support the direct payments made by the federal government to farmers; consumers pay additional sums to farmers through the higher prices that result from acreage restrictions and other supply management techniques. Aside from the administrative costs involved, these amounts transferred from consumers and taxpayers to farmers do not represent a loss of national income, merely a redistribution of it. But there are, nevertheless, national income costs (or welfare losses) associated with the farm price support programs, arising from the diversion of resources caused by acreage restrictions that leads to a reduction in national income (or the national welfare). These national income costs are smaller than the transfer costs associated with the programs.

Figures A-1 and A-2, in a highly simplified fashion, illustrate the difference between the two kinds of costs.

In Figure A-1 the nationwide demand and supply (marginal cost) curves for a particular farm commodity are shown as DD and MC_1, respectively. With no farm price support programs in existence, amount Q_0 would be produced and sold at price P_0. If, now, price support objective P_1 is established, production must somehow be cut to Q_1. Otherwise the government will have to buy, and hold off the market, the amount $Q_2 - Q_1$ (that is, at price P_1 farmers will produce Q_2, of which only Q_1 can be disposed of in the marketplace).

Figure A-2 depicts the situation after the introduction of "voluntary" acreage restriction programs, designed to restrict production to level Q_1, consistent with price support objective P_1.[1] Farmers who agree to reduce their planted acreage by a certain percentage receive direct payments from the government. Since acreage is restricted, the cost of producing any given quantity of the farm commodity rises; more fertilizer or pesticide or labor must be applied to the

1. In actuality, because direct payments under the voluntary acreage restriction program contribute to farm income, the market price objective P_1 can be, and is, lower than in the purchase situation depicted in Fig. A-1.

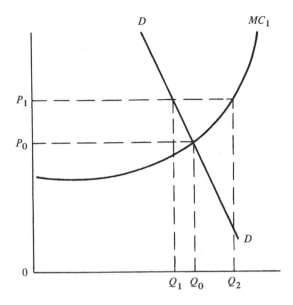

Figure A-1. Effect of Price Supports on Farm Production

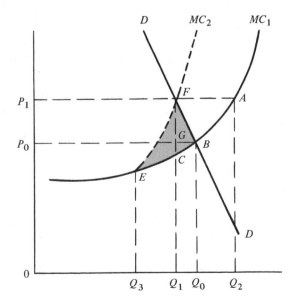

Figure A-2. National Income Costs with price Supports and Supply Controls

remaining acres. The result is the new supply (marginal cost) curve MC_2 shown in Figure A-2. The trick is to induce enough acreage reductions to make the new cost curve cut the demand curve at the desired price and quantity combination (P_1, Q_1).

Participation in the acreage restriction programs is voluntary; that is, any farmer may decide not to restrict his acreage and forgo receiving payments as well as giving up the privilege of putting his crop under a Commodity Credit Corporation (CCC) loan.[2] From the viewpoint of the individual farmer, his participation in the program will depend upon whether the direct payments are large enough to compensate him for the income he might have earned by *not* restricting acreage and producing out to the point where his marginal cost curve cuts the new price line P_1. For all producers taken together, the amount of income loss that must be compensated through direct payments is the area $ABCEF$ in Figure A-2. As a matter of fact, however, the Department of Agriculture must set its direct payment formula high enough to generate an aggregate volume of payments larger than $ABCEF$, if it wishes to induce enough participation to shift production back to Q_1. Only if it could calculate, farm by farm, the income loss associated with acreage restrictions could it achieve a direct payment aggregate as low as $ABCEF$. But lack of data, political considerations, and administrative limitations make this impossible. Rather, with minor qualifications, it must set a common direct payment formula for all producers. This means that the formula must be set high enough to attract the marginal participants, and therefore substantially higher than absolutely necessary to attract the bulk of participants.[3] As a consequence, the sums transferred to farmers by taxpayers, via direct payments, will be equal to area $ABCEF$ plus a substantial additional sum, whose magnitude basically depends on the degree to which marginal cost curves differ among individual farmers.[4]

The consumer loses a sum equal to the area P_1FBP_0, of which P_1FGP_0 is transferred to the farmer and FGB is lost altogether (part of the national income loss discussed below).

Total transfer costs are therefore equal to the higher prices paid by consumers on the amount they consume (area P_1FGP_0) and the amount paid by

2. The latter privilege is generally valuable to the farmer because the actual market price may fall below the target (or "loan") price P_1—that is, the government may miscalculate—and the CCC loan allows the farmer more flexibility in determining when to market his crop.

3. In technical jargon the Department of Agriculture cannot act as a discriminating monopsonist in buying participation. It must set a common price for all.

4. Actually the department sometimes indulges in limited payment discrimination. In some years, and for some commodities, a two-layer payment scheme is offered: all participants are required to reduce acreage by a specified percentage and are thereby entitled to a specified amount of direct payments; in addition, participants may choose to retire still further acreage and receive payments based on the added acreage. The two levels of payment are different, the second level being lower and designed to attract out of production land on which the difference between price and cost is not very large—that is, the income loss to be compensated is not very great.

taxpayers in the form of direct payments (area *ABCEF* plus an additional sum necessitated by the inability of the program to discriminate in its payments).

The transfer costs of the program do not represent a loss of national output or welfare, but a redistribution of it. There are net losses to the society from the program, however. These are measured by the shaded area *FBCE*. For each unit of output lost $(Q_0 - Q_1)$ there was an excess of what consumers were willing to pay over the additional cost of that unit—that is, the difference between the demand curve and the marginal cost curve. The loss of welfare on the lost output is therefore the area *FCB*. In addition, on part of the output actually produced, marginal costs are higher. These additional costs are represented by area *FCE*. The sum of the two losses—the welfare loss on the output that would otherwise have been produced and the cost increase for the output actually produced—is the total national income loss, *FBCE*.

This diagrammatic presentation necessarily makes a number of simplifications and leaves out several important points:

1. It ignores the problem of exports. A significant proportion of price-supported products are exported. To some extent the foreign, not the American, consumer pays the transfer costs described above. But foreign tariff mechanisms (for example, variable "gate levies") are often such that changes in prices of American agricultural exports result not in price changes to foreign consumers but in changes in tariff revenue collected by foreign governments.

2. The price support programs provide a higher, more stable set of prices for farmers than would free markets. It is often asserted that the existence of relatively high and stable prices has stimulated the growth of productivity on farms, particularly through a faster acceptance of new techniques and a higher rate of investment than would otherwise have been the case. Even with acreage restrictions, farm costs may be lower rather than higher than they would be in a free market. Hence the diagram overstates the national income losses (part of which stem from higher costs). Whatever the validity of this position, it is a strange argument to use in defense of a program whose very existence is based on the proposition that the growth of farm productivity so far outstrips the growth of demand for farm products as to require price support and supply restrictions.

3. The price support programs provide not only high prices but stable prices (at least relative to the volatility of farm prices in a free market). This price stability in turn is a benefit to the farmer and should be counted as an offset to the national income losses shown in the diagram. While this point has undeniable merit, it immediately raises the question of whether or not relatively stable prices could not be provided at lower average levels. Some of the national income losses associated with high price supports could thus be avoided, and some protection would be available against the extreme swings of free agriculture markets.

Methodology for Distributing the Benefits
of Farm Commodity Programs by Economic Class

From background data underlying the Economic Research Service's (ERS) 1968 model of the farm economy,[1] estimates were made of the change in cash receipts resulting from the removal of price supports and production controls for the period 1961-67 for the following commodity groups: wheat, feed grains, cotton, sugar, all other crops, and livestock. A decline in the prices of feed grains and livestock would, of course, reduce the production expenses of livestock producers, who purchase feed and livestock; the estimated change in livestock cash receipts is a net figure, after adjustment for the decline in feed grain and purchased livestock expenses.

Production expenses, aside from purchased feed and livestock, do not change sharply when price supports are removed. For the 1961-67 period as a whole, production expenses would have declined by $2 billion, of which $1.5 billion is accounted for by purchased feed and livestock. Hence the fall in cash receipts, adjusted for a drop in the cost of purchased feed and livestock, is a reasonably good approximation of the fall in net income.[2]

The decline in adjusted cash receipts was apportioned to each economic class, I through VI, on the basis of 1964 census value-of-production data. Farmers in each economic class were assumed to have received benefits from price supports in proportion to their production of the particular crop involved. Or to say this another way, the distribution of the value of production for each commodity group was calculated, and then the various distributions were combined with weights based upon the free market decline in adjusted cash receipts for the particular commodity or group.

The value-of-production data used for the distribution were not taken raw from the census. They were first adjusted to control totals based on the cash receipts figures for each economic class published annually by ERS in *Farm*

1. See pp. 22-25 for a discussion of the model. The data were supplied by M. L. Upchurch, administrator, and W. B. Sundquist, director of the Farm Production Economics Division, of the Economic Research Service of the U.S. Department of Agriculture.
2. There are also changes in noncash items of income, chiefly the value of food produced and consumed on the farm. But these are relatively minor.

Income Situation. As a consequence, the value-of-production data used in the individual commodity distributions, when summed for each economic class, equal the ERS published figures on the cash receipts of that economic class.

Weighting the individual commodity distributions across economic classes by the free market decline in adjusted cash receipts produces an aggregate percentage distribution of price support benefits for each economic class. In turn this was applied to the ERS estimate of the aggregate decline in cash receipts, excluding government payments, to arrive at an aggregate dollar value of price support benefits for each class.

In effect the ERS measure of the decline in adjusted cash receipts for the various commodities serves as a rough measure of price support benefits for the period as a whole; those benefits are distributed by economic class according to the 1964 share of each economic class in the total production of each relevant commodity.

One apparently peculiar feature of the calculation is the very low value of price support benefits to livestock producers. This stems from the fact that in the first several years of the 1961-67 period, free market conditions would bring about a reduction in prices for feed. But production of livestock would not immediately rise in response to lower feed prices, and for some time prices of livestock would not decline. Facing roughly unchanged cash receipts and lower feed prices, livestock producers would temporarily enjoy a rise in income. As production was raised in response to these conditions, prices would eventually fall, and the income of livestock producers would be reduced. The ERS model for the later years of the period does reflect a decline in livestock income. But averaged for the 1961-67 period as a whole, livestock producers' incomes would have been unchanged.

Comparison of Direct Payments with Price Support Benefits

One fact stands out from the distribution of benefits: the distribution of direct payments is somewhat less concentrated among larger farmers than is the distribution of price support benefits (see Tables 7 and 8). The wheat, feed grain, and agricultural conservation program subsidies are responsible for the differences.

In 1964 the major direct payment programs were in wheat and feed grains. For these crops, production is much less concentrated among large producers than it is, on the average, for other farm commodities. Hence, even if wheat and feed grain direct payments were distributed among economic classes in proportion to their production of these crops, the aggregate distribution of direct payments would be less concentrated among large producers than is the case with price support benefits. Table B-1 contrasts the distribution of benefits for the major crops with a distribution in which price support bene-

Table B-1. Distribution of Price Support Benefits and Direct Payments, 1964
Percent

	Economic class					
Distribution	*I*	*II*	*III*	*IV*	*V*	*VI*
Price support benefits	42.3	19.3	17.9	11.0	5.3	4.2
Price support benefits for wheat, feed grains, sugar, and wool, based on direct payment weights	24.3	25.8	26.9	14.4	5.3	3.2
Direct payments[a]	14.7	20.4	26.6	17.5	8.7	12.1

Source: Based on data from U.S. Department of Agriculture (USDA), Economic Research Service, *Farm Income Situation,* FIS-216 (July 1970); USDA, Agricultural Stabilization and Conservation Service, *Sugar Statistics and Related Data Compiled in the Administration of the U.S. Sugar Acts,* Vol. 2 (revised; February 1969); and unpublished Department of Agriculture data.
a. These figures differ from those in Table 7 because they have not been adjusted to include cotton payments.

fits for each crop were weighted by direct payment weights. This artificial aggregate distribution asks the question: "Suppose price support benefits had been distributed among crops in 1964 the same way direct payment benefits were distributed; wheat and feed grains received most of the benefits; what would the resulting aggregate distribution of price benefits look like?" As the table shows, the heavy weight of the relatively "unconcentrated" wheat and feed grains would reduce the overall concentration of benefits.

Within the wheat and feed grains categories, benefits are not distributed in accordance with production of those crops. The proportion of both very large and very small farmers who participate in these programs is less than the participating ratio among farmers in the middle of the spectrum. This is particularly noticeable in the feed grain program, as Table B-2 indicates.

As explained on page 14, the direct payment total used in this study includes the agricultural conservation program (ACP) subsidies. ACP is not

Table B-2. Wheat and Feed Grain Farms with Land in Diversion Programs, 1964
Percent

	Economic class						*All*
Program	*I*	*II*	*III*	*IV*	*V*	*VI*[a]	*farms*
Wheat	33.1	35.7	36.5	36.6	27.1	13.6	32.4
Feed grains	39.1	51.0	50.0	46.3	35.8	21.5	43.4

Source: U.S. Bureau of the Census, *Census of Agriculture, 1964, Statistics by Subjects,* Vol. 2, Chap. 10: *Type of Farm* (1964), Table 9, pp. 1012, 1013.
a. Commercial farms only.

tied to commodity production and is much more evenly distributed than the direct payments under the commodity program (see Table 3).

Comparison of the Distributions of Price Support Benefits and Net Income

The distribution of price support benefits is more heavily concentrated among higher economic class farms than is the distribution of net income (see Table B-3). As pointed out on page 17, the net income from farming of small farmers is a much higher proportion of cash receipts than is that of large farmers. Consequently, a given increase in price supports yields a greater share of benefits to larger farmers than their share of total net income.

Table B-3. Distribution of Price Support Benefits and Net Income, 1964 and 1969

Percent

Distribution and year	*Economic class*					
	I	*II*	*III*	*IV*	*V*	*VI*
Price support benefits						
1964	42.3	19.3	17.9	11.0	5.3	4.2
1969	52.9	21.0	15.4	6.1	2.2	2.4
Net income[a]						
1964	26.0	19.5	22.0	14.1	7.1	11.3
1969	35.9	23.1	20.3	8.7	3.8	8.2

Source: Price support benefits from Tables 7 and 8; net income from *Farm Income Situation,* July 1970, p. 71.
a. Including off-farm income.

Moreover, only a small fraction of the total income of many small farmers comes, on the average, from farm sources. Typically, a large fraction comes from such off-farm sources as part-time work and retirement income. A given percentage increase in farm income affects them relatively less than it affects large farmers. Table B-4 suggests the importance of this factor.

Table B-4. Sources of Farmers' Income, by Economic Class, 1964 and 1969

Economic class	Year	Income per farmer (dollars)			Off-farm as percentage of total
		On-farm	*Off-farm*	*Total*	
I	1964	23,301	3,959	27,260	15
	1969	27,503	5,464	32,967	17
II	1964	9,531	2,313	11,844	20
	1969	10,466	3,241	13,707	24
III	1964	5,989	2,062	8,047	26
	1969	6,481	3,141	9,622	33
IV	1964	3,464	2,827	6,291	45
	1969	3,630	4,488	8,118	55
V	1964	1,973	3,064	5,037	61
	1969	2,122	4,895	7,017	70
VI	1964	954	4,139	5,093	81
	1969	1,082	7,011	8,093	87

Source: *Farm Income Situation,* July 1970, p. 72.

The Influence of Urban Development
on Farmland Prices

The long-run rise in farmland prices is apparently explainable by increasing returns to farmland. For this and a number of other reasons, the hypothesis that a large part of the rise in farmland prices results from the pressure of urban expansion is unwarranted.

Some 70 percent of farmland purchases in recent years have been made by farmers who plan to farm the acquired land. Of the remaining 30 percent, 20 percent went to buyers who planned to rent the land to someone else for farm operations. Some 2.5 percent of purchases were made by persons seeking a rural residence and only 6.5 percent for possibly speculative purposes.[1] Clearly, some of the 20 percent of purchasers who intended to rent the land for farm use may also have been primarily speculators, hoping for a capital gain from eventual urban expansion. Nevertheless, it would appear that purchases for immediate developmental purposes were only a small part of the total market. These figures do not, of course, prove that urban development played no role in forcing up farmland prices. They do show, however, that most farmland was purchased for farm use.

Allan Schmid, in an extensive study of the conversion of land from rural to urban use,[2] found that the price received by farmers on urban fringes for land to be used in urban development was very much greater than the average value of farmland in the state within which the particular city was located. Using data for 259 cities, he found that farmland with an average statewide value of $300 was sold by the last farm owner for $1,300 when the land was to be converted to urban uses. This huge disparity between average state land values and urban fringe values implies that the urban-use value of farmland quickly tapers off as one moves beyond the urban fringe into the rural areas

1. U.S. Department of Agriculture, Economic Research Service, *Farm Real Estate Market Developments*, CD-69 (June 1967), Tables 14 and 17, pp. 20, 23.
2. A. Allan Schmid, *Converting Land from Rural to Urban Uses* (Johns Hopkins Press for Resources for the Future, 1968).

where the great bulk of farmland exists. In other words, the great bulk of farmland prices are determined by the value of land in farm use.

As another rough check, the increase in farmland prices between 1963 and 1967 for the major farming regions was correlated with the 1966-67 ratio between returns to land and farmland values. The hypothesis was that farmland values would rise most where returns were high relative to land prices—that is, the change in the price of land represented a movement to restore equality between the price of land and the capitalized value of land rent. This was admittedly an extremely crude test, relying upon readily available data.[3] Yet the interregional variation in the land return–land price ratio explained 61 percent of the variance in regional land price increases. The pattern of deviations of actual land price increases from those estimated in the regression did not suggest any regular influence of urbanization. Among areas with large land price increases relative to those predicted from the regression were the Appalachian, Corn Belt, and Delta regions. The three areas with the lowest rate of land price increases relative to the regression were the Southeast, the Northern Plains, and the Mountain States.

The above considerations are by no means conclusive. But when combined with the fact that farmland prices have risen over the long run by the same percentage as farmland rents, they do suggest that urbanization does not account for the rapid rise in farmland prices.

3. Regional returns to land were presented by Bruce B. Johnson, "An Active Land Market in Perspective," *Farm Real Estate Market Developments,* CD-71 (December 1968), Table 2, p. 31. Regional farmland prices were obtained from *Farm Real Estate Market Developments,* CD-70 (April 1968), Table 25, pp. 42-43.

DATE DUE

MAY 20 '76			
MAR 29 '77			
MAR 17 '77			
MAR 6 '79			
MAR 16 '79			
OCT 1 6 '79			
NOV 11 79			
NOV 3 '79			
NOV 1 0 1981			
JAN 26 '82			
JAN 8 1982			
MAY 1 0 1983			
MAY 1 0 1983			
MAR 11 '86			
FEB 1 3 '96			
DEC 2 0 '96			
GAYLORD			PRINTED IN U.S.A.